GIAN M

On the trail of the Shroud

Early and recent history

Translated by Alan Neame

ST PAULS

Series: THE SHROUD OF TURIN

1. Shroud, Gospels and Christian life.
2. The Shroud under the microscope. Forensic examination.
3. On the trail of the Shroud. Early and recent history.
4. An 'inexplicable' image. Theories on how the image on the Shroud was formed.
5. The image on the Shroud. Results of photography and information technology.
6. Shroud, carbon dating and calculus of probabilities.
7. Myrrh, aloes, pollen and other traces. Botanical research on the Shroud.

On the front cover: *St Charles Borromeo venerating the Shroud* by Giacomo & Giovanni Andrea Casella (Church of San Carlo, Turin, c. 1655).

ST PAULS
Ireland
London SW1P 1EP, United Kingdom

© ST PAULS (UK) 1998

ISBN 085439 534 2

Set by TuKan, High Wycombe
Produced in the EC
Printed by The Guernsey Press Co. Ltd, Guernsey, C.I.

ST PAULS is an activity of the priests and brothers of the Society of St Paul who proclaim the Gospel through the media of social communication

CONTENTS

BIBLIOGRAPHICAL NOTE

Writings and lectures on the history of the Shroud abound; this whole booklet would not be able to contain a complete bibliography. Without any claim to completeness and of necessity leaving out texts just as, if not even more, important, here are some works which the reader may consult who wishes to delve deeper into what has been said here. A general treatment of the Shroud's history will be found in I. Wilson, *The Turin Shroud*, London 1978. For its ancient history, see A. M. Dubarle, *Histoire ancienne du linceul de Turin, jusq' au XIII siècle*, Paris 1985, and the various writings of G. Zaninotto in the *Acts* of the Sindonological Congresses; in *Sindon*, the review published by the International Centre of Sindonology, Turin; and in *Collegamento pro Sindone*, a supplement to *Collegamento pro Fidelitate*, Rome, a work which may also be consulted for a more general background. A rich collection of documents is to be found in P. Savio, *Ricerche storiche sulla Santa Sindone*, Turin 1957. For the later period, see A. Perret, *Essai sur l'histoire du Saint-Suaire du XIV au XVI siècle*, in 'Mémoires de l'Académie des Sciences, Belles Lettres et Arts de Savoiel sixth series, vol. IV (1960). On the happenings at Lirey, see L. Fossati, *La Santa Sindone, nuova luce su antichi documenti*, Turin 1961. Essential for iconography, its limitations notwithstanding, is P. Vignon, *Le Saint-Suaire de Turin devant la science, l'archéologie, l'histoire, l'iconographie. la logique*, Paris 1938, and the up to the minute W. Bulst, H. Pfeiffer, *Das Turiner Grabtuch und das Christusbild*, Frankfurt 1987-1991. For an essay against the authenticity of the Shroud, based on historical theories, see V. Saxer, *La Sindone di Torino e la storia*, in 'Rivista di storia della Chiesa in Italia', XLIII, 1 (January – June 1989).

Foreword

The earliest book about the Shroud

In 1578 the Duke of Savoy charged Emmanuel Philibert Pingone, Baron de Cusy, with the task of writing what was to be the first book entirely devoted to the Shroud. After three years' work Pingone printed a booklet almost exclusively devoted to the Shroud's history. Despite the possibility of access to the Savoyard archives and the relative closeness in time of some of the events described, he had to fall back on imagination and somewhat forced reconstructions to take the Shroud's history back to the tomb of Jesus.

The 'historical' problem of the Shroud is of

very long standing and even today we have to admit that, remarkable acquisitions of knowledge notwithstanding, we have not progressed very far from the basic problems encountered by Pingone in the sixteenth century, although certain advances, even important ones, have of course been made.

In the following pages, even so, we shall try to work out an itinerary taking us back as far in time as possible, our starting point – forwards and backwards in time – being the middle of the fourteenth century when the Shroud first made its appearance in Europe, since when we have never lost sight of it.

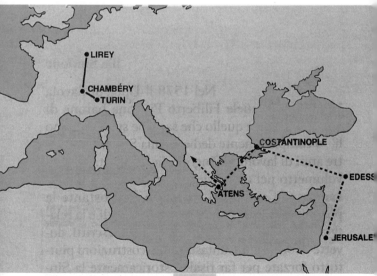

Map showing the travels of the Shroud, those documented and those presumed.

The Shroud at Lirey

The noble knight
Geoffroy de Charny

The vicissitudes of the Shroud on its appearance in Europe towards the middle of the fourteenth century are closely linked to the history of the house of De Charny, a noble Burgundian family with pretty influential kinsfolk.

The member of this family with whom we begin is Geoffroy de Charny who, at the time, was one of the most prominent figures in the kingdom of France, a valiant knight and a man of deep faith. Among expressions of his piety, the most outstanding was his building of a church in his fief at Lirey under the title of the Annunciation of the Virgin Mary, which was completed in 1353.

It was in this church that Geoffroy deposited the Shroud, presumably between its foundation and his death, which occurred heroically in battle on September 19, 1356. We do not have documents to establish the exact date, nor is there a precise tradition as to how Geoffroy de Charny came into possession of a relic of such importance.

Its authenticity first contested

Paradoxically the historical circumstances of the period are handed down to us in a group of contemporary documents, among which is a writing from the end of the fourteenth century drawn up by the Bishop of Troyes, Pierre d'Arcis, to whose diocese Lirey belonged – which is totally opposed to the Shroud's authenticity. The document states that the Shroud is an artefact, the maker of which will soon be discovered and named. Such swindles had already been unmasked by Pierre d'Arcis's predecessor, Bishop Henri de Poitiers, immediately after the first expositions, he being alarmed by the extraordinary throng of devotees. D'Arcis's memorial goes on to say that the Canons of Lirey had then withdrawn the relic, only to reinstate it in the church some 35 years later, at the very time when Pierre d'Arcis was writing, and when Geoffroy II de Charny, son of the foregoing, had obtained permission for this, not from the Bishop of Troyes, but from the Papal Legate, Pierre de Tury.

This was going over Pierre d'Arcis's head. He reacted immediately and, taking his stand on the fact that the Canons had extended the Legate's concession (which was limited to letting the Shroud be kept in church) to the right to exhibit it as well, forbade expositions on pain of excommunication.

Clement VII intervenes

The documents in our possession allow us to reconstruct a fair part of what happened between 1389 and 1390. The parties appealed to the King of France, Charles VI, who, despite having allowed the celebration of expositions by earlier measures, ordered the Sheet to be confiscated. One may think that having a valid reason, such as the Bishop's request, for taking possession of the Shroud – an object kept in a church and of widespread fame – might have inclined the Sovereign's will to the Bishop's argument. If the 'coup' had gone right, the history of the Shroud might have taken a very different course. The Canons however refused to hand the Shroud over, and the case was referred to the papal authority in the person of Clement VII, the Avignonese anti-pope (1378-1394) known in the world as Robert of Geneva. Faced with so thorny a situation where religious, political and even family interests were all mixed up together, Clement VII found an obviously compromise solution, by imposing silence on the Bishop and authorising the expositions, which however were to be held without solemnity, accompanied by the explicit declaration that this was not the real Shroud of Jesus but one of its ill-defined 'representations'. For the odd thing is, it seems clear from the vagueness with which the Shroud is described that none of the principal actors in this business – apart of course from the Canons and the de Charny family had ever seen the Shroud but were speaking from hearsay or from the reports of others.

Limitations of Pierre d'Arcis's memorial

This was what happened at Lirey, over which rivers of ink have flowed and which sometimes even today is invoked as final by those who deny the Shroud's authenticity.

It is an event reconstructed on the strength of documents which, although significant in themselves, are nonetheless full of gaps, leaving many questions unanswered as to how precisely things developed and giving us to suppose that other papers existed but are now lost. Here we witness the adopting of very fluctuating positions, even on the part of the Pope, who a few months later was to modify the text of his measure in a sense less unfavourable than that appearing in the first version, and then to begin granting indulgences to people visiting the church in actual consideration of the fact the Shroud was preserved in it.

But no matter how firmly based Pierre d'Arcis's memorial may be, we must still point out its objective limitations as regards the scope of what it covers. For it seems the only person who had even bothered to have the Shroud studied with a view to drawing conclusions about it had been Henri de Poitiers, but of these inspections no documentary records exist. Pierre d'Arcis is the only person to mention them years later in a writing which, to say the least, is somewhat peculiar in the way it is drafted and which, at least in the form known to us, does not seem likely to have been – frankly indeed, never could have been – submitted to the papal court.

On the other hand it emerges pretty clearly that the important problem of authenticity is being used as a stalking horse: the real nub of the matter is essentially liturgical and hierarchical. We should also bear in mind when subjecting documents to critical evaluation that distinction must be drawn between formal authenticity and historical truth of the content – in the sense that a document may be authentic, i.e. dating back to the period in question and drawn up in such a way as completely to express the author's thought, and yet for various reasons may contain untrue statements. In our case therefore, the memorial, however authentic it may be, may contain statements vitiated by poor knowledge of the facts. In any case, research carried out on the Shroud has completely ruled out a painted origin for the imprint, and the certainty that the sheet analysed is the same as the one venerated and quarrelled over at Lirey brings down the load-bearing pillar of Pierre d'Arcis's thesis.

Marguerite de Charny and the House of Savoy

Travels of the Shroud across Europe

Geoffroy de Charny's family did not have a long history. The only descendant we find still alive in the 1400s was Marguerite, daughter of Geoffroy II, who took as her second husband Humbert de La Roche.

She was left a widow again in 1438, still without issue. It isn't hard to imagine the complexities a lady on her own might face in the legal and social conditions of the day.

We find traces of Marguerite in various parts of Europe, clearly seeking somewhere to settle down.

She is alone, but with her she takes what she regards as a great treasure and this she guards with stubborn determination while trying understandably enough to make use of it to improve her own situation. This is of course the Shroud, which Humbert de La Roche had taken away from the church at Lirey on July 6, 1418, with other relics and valuables, as a precaution against wartime marauders. The receipt for these articles still survives, in which Humbert promises to return them when the dangers are over.

A return that never took place, notwithstanding the repeated injunctions of the Canons, who took Marguerite to court several times. Lawsuits, covenants and adjournments up to the excommunication pronounced in 1457 document Marguerite's wanderings, with extemporary expositions of the Shroud, the outcomes of which were at times contrary to expectations, as was the case at Chimay where in 1449 she was pressed to exhibit the documents proving the relic's authenticity and could only present the doubtful decisions of the antipope Clement VII.

Cession to the Dukes of Savoy

At last her peregrinations brought her to the court of the dukes of Savoy, to which furthermore Humbert de La Roche was in some way connected.

In Geneva in 1453 the Shroud was transferred to the House of Savoy.

The date has been long debated, for, lacking the document directly relating to the cession, we cannot go back to the day, even less to the conditions, on which the transfer was made. There does however exist a series of documents dated between 1453 and 1455 which bear witness to a notable volume of business between Duke Louis of Savoy and Marguerite de Charny, involving financial matters but also very complex feudal ones, in which a curious personage also takes part: François de La Palud – a footloose knight who managed to get himself banished from Savoyan territory – who was in some way Humbert's heir and whom some ancient bibliographical sources name as the person through whom the Shroud came to the Savoys.

Of these documents the first ones date from March 22, 1453, the date traditionally held (on the basis of Pingonel's information) to be that of the cession. In these documents however there is no specific mention of the Shroud and probably neither could there be. For the transfer was certainly of dubious validity, involving as it did a *quid pro quo*. Hence the existence of an official deed is hardly thinkable, documenting the cession – of validity even more dubious – of a sacred object by a person whose actual ownership of the object was being disputed.

Be that as it may, from that date the Shroud began to be part of the patrimony of the House of Savoy (which went on defending its own rights to it until 1983, when by his will the last and exiled King of Italy, Umberto II bequeathed it to the Holy See in the person of the Sovereign Pontiff), and to the Canons of Lirey, having lost all hope of being able to compete with the powerful House of Savoy, nothing remained but to be content with an annual pension bestowed by the Duke of Savoy on February 6, 1464.

Further travels before landing at Chambéry

But if the widening renown and devotion to the Shroud began with this change of ownership, its vicissitudes were by no means over. For in the earliest period the Savoys insisted on always having with them what they from the outset held to be the most precious relic in Christendom. And so the Shroud followed the court on progress to its various castles: shut in a chest where it was kept folded up to take less room, to make it easier to move and to render it less conspicuous. Thus for the first time known, the Shroud entered Piedmont in 1477, with a probable exposition at Pinerolo in 1478, then again in 1488 and yet again in 1494 at Vercelli. In 1495 it was exposed in Turin.

In view of the need to give the Shroud a fixed abode, it was eventually transferred with great pomp on June 11, 1502, to the Sainte-Chapelle forming part of Chambéry castle. Nonetheless we have to wait until 1506 before this arrangement became permanent. 1506 was important for another reason, since at the request of Duke Charles III and his mother Claude de Bresse of Brittany approval was granted for the public veneration and liturgical office of the Shroud. Its feast-day was set on May 4, and the title of 'Sainte-Chapelle of the Holy Shroud' was conferred on the Chambéry chapel. In the relevant Bull, Pope Julius II uses expressions which apparently entertain no doubts about the Shroud's authenticity.

The fierce fire of 1532 and the 'recognition' of 1534

On the night of December 4, 1532, in this chapel a violent fire broke out, vividly described by Pingone, and this very nearly destroyed the Shroud. The damage caused on this occasion is well known and still visible today under the patches the Poor Clares were charged with sewing on the Shroud in 1534. At the same time, to strengthen the fabric, they applied a Holland backing which still covers the back of the Shroud today. We have a record of this operation in an extraordinarily touching document (now lost but printed in the 1800s) written with piety and devotion by the Sisters.

Following this incident, the customary exposition of May 4 was not celebrated in 1533, feeding rumours that the Shroud had been destroyed in the fire. An echo of these rumours can be heard in Rabelais' *Gargantua*. To quieten the rumours Pope Clement VII (the proper one, Giulio de' Medici, 1523-1534) was petitioned and in turn decreed that an official commission of recognition should be set up under the presidency of the Cardinal Legate, Louis de Gorrevod, who knew the Shroud well, having himself petitioned Rome for the institution of its public veneration.

The 'recognition' took place on April 15, 1534, in the presence of twelve witnesses, among whom were three bishops and the President of the Chamber of Nobles, who swore that what was submitted to their eyes was that same Shroud as was venerated before the fire. In any case it would have been very difficult to deceive the vast numbers of people who each year and on each occasion flocked to the expositions.

The Shroud in Milan, Nice and Vercelli

But other woes were about to overtake the House of Savoy, and these interrupted the Shroud's stay in Chambéry. Duke Charles III found himself caught up in the great political machine which in those days was dividing Europe and by which he was crushed. Chased out by the French who in 1536 were to occupy Chambéry and then Turin, he abandoned his dominions, taking the Shroud with him. After long wanderings which eventually brought him to Milan, where an exposition was held in that same year, he reached Nice as his final refuge in 1537. These were very sad times for the State of Savoy which was virtually on its last legs, most of its territory having been occupied and divided between the French and Spanish.

Charles III then settled in Vercelli, where he died during the night of August 16-17, 1553, and – final insult – was robbed of his personal jewels. The Shroud had been placed in a side-chapel of Vercelli Cathedral, from which, three months after the Duke's death, it was nearly carried off by French troops who had taken the city by surprise. The presence of mind and courage of one of the canons of the cathedral, Giovanni Antonio Costa, saved the relic in that particular crisis. The Shroud returned to Chambéry in 1561 at the wish of the new duke Emmanuel Philibert, who by the Treaty of Cateau-Cambrésis had obtained the restitution of part of the lands that his father had lost.

The Shroud and the House of Savoy

With Emmanuel Philibert, the House of Savoy's glory days began. Time was ripe for a fresh start in Savoyard polity. Under the driving force of the young, decisive ruler, institutions developed in the direction of an absolute state, while strategic interests were channelled towards the Italian peninsula. The consequence of this was the displacement of the centre of command from Chambéry to Turin, which was better suited to the new requirements. Having changed the political and administrative centre, the only thing still lacking was the religious 'sign': the Shroud.

Much has been said about the Savoys' 'political' exploitation of the Shroud. For as soon as it came into their possession, they got its cult approved, spread knowledge of it and promoted study of it. Exposition was to accompany all the most important moments in their family life: accession to the throne, marriages, baptisms. Yet it is not correct to hold that the Shroud was used unscrupulously as an instrument of power. Rather, it was regarded, in the doctrinal context of the times, as a sign of the favour of God – the fountainhead of all authority – for the ruling house, conferring on it a privileged position among other houses far more powerful and more ancient. It was hence (if you will) rather a matter of 'image', underpinned however by sincere devotion at all levels from sovereign to populace. The Shroud became the 'protection' of the family and of the state against adversities, in hard times of pestilence and wars, and a means of praising and thanking God on occasions for rejoicing. In the days of Emmanuel Philibert, the Shroud-image fluttered above the flagship of the little Piedmontese fleet at the Battle of Lepanto (1571), while the trophy offered by the Commune of Turin as *ex-voto* for cessation of the plague in 1630 was set into the altar of the Chapel of the Shroud.

The Shroud in Turin

The Shroud reached Turin on September 14, 1578, amid the roar of cannon, and was received with high solemnity. Getting it away from Chambéry had been far from easy. Emmanuel Philibert was obliged to find some plausible excuse for shifting the relic, well aware of negative reactions in the capital of Savoy but also worried about the dangers it might run there. His opportunity came when Carlo Borromeo expressed the desire to make a pilgrimage on foot to venerate the Shroud and fulfil a vow made during the plague of 1576. To shorten the prelate's journey – for he was well-known and already reputed a saint – was justification to which even the Canons of Chambéry had to yield. They tried to safeguard their interests, insisting on a formal assurance that it was only to be a temporary removal. In vain: once having left Chambéry and secretly reached Turin via the Little St Bernard, Aosta, Ivrea, Ciriè and Lucento, the Shroud was never to return to Savoy.

Carlo Borromeo finished his pilgrimage after a four days' walk in torrential rain. On October 10, 1578, he was able to venerate the Shroud in a private exposition and several times publicly on the days following.

Various temporary arrangements were made for the Shroud in Turin until, in 1587, it was placed in the shrine raised aloft on four pillars and built for it, before the old choir of the Cathedral, roughly in the area corresponding to the present choir and hence towering over the high altar. Here it remained until May 1685 when it was moved to the Chapel of Saints Stephen and Catherine at the bottom of the left-hand aisle, to allow the building of the new structure designed by Guarino Guarini, to which it was finally translated on June 1, 1694.

The permanent installation of the Shroud in Turin was marked by expositions on every May 4 and others on special occasions to celebrate dynastic events as we have already said, but also to mark the presence in Turin of important personalities or to solemnise extraordinary events, such as to thank God for the ending of the civil war between the 'Principists' and the 'Madamists', when the Municipality sent its own standard into the field, bearing the Shroud-image on it.

Studying the Shroud begins

With its arrival in Turin, studies of the Shroud began, only in part commissioned by the Savoys, for the geographical distribution of the writings about it bears witness to its wide renown and the interest and curiosity it aroused. In the sixteenth and seventeenth centuries more than a hundred publications appeared which in differing forms and contexts treated of the relic – from brief notices to whole books devoted to it.

When the Shroud was transferred in 1694, it was also decided to change the cover which normally protected it, and Blessed Sebastian Valfré was granted the honour of repairing certain frayed points in the fabric. Valfré, today a little remembered representative of Turinese sanctity, had a very special devotion to the Shroud and devoted his whole life to promoting devotion to it, regarding it as a privileged instrument for meditation on Christ's passion and a direct spur to love of one's neighbour. Valfré, who was very close to the people and the court, was indeed a tireless promoter of charity in the city, above all in moments of crisis, as for example in 1706 when Turin endured a prolonged and exhausting siege during which the famous incident of Pietro Micca occurred.

That siege was one of the only two occasions when the Shroud left the city. For it travelled with the ducal family first to Oneglia and thence by sea to Genoa. Victor Amadeus II alone stayed in Turin to organise resistance and await the imperial reinforcements commanded by his cousin Prince Eugene of Savoy-Soissons.

By strange coincidence the Shroud in the capital of Liguria was given shelter in a palace quite close to the church of St Bartholomew of the

Armenians, where a venerated picture of the *Mandylion* of Edessa was and still is preserved to this day. We shall shortly be seeing the importance of this *Mandylion* in the history of the Shroud.

Back once more in Turin, the Shroud was not to leave the city again for many years, for during the period of French occupation the Savoys took refuge in Sardinia, leaving the Shroud in its chapel, in the Archbishop's custody.

Expositions in the nineteenth century

The return of the rightful sovereigns to their dominions was naturally celebrated with an exposition on May 20, 1814. We have no record of any public expositions during the French occupation.

Instead we know of two private ones: the first in 1799 when the Archbishop of Turin wished to check the state of the Shroud on making himself responsible for it; and a second, very special one in 1804 in the presence of Pope Pius VII who stopped in Turin on his journey to crown Napoleon. Eleven years later, during the period of the 'Hundred Days', this same pope was once again in Turin, where he took part in a solemn public exposition on May 25, 1815.

The custom of regular expositions having lapsed, there were fewer opportunities for seeing the Shroud in the nineteenth century. After the exposition of 1822 ordered by Charles Felix to invoke Heaven's protection at the beginning of his reign, we have records of one in 1842 to mark the marriage of the future Victor Emmanuel II and Maria Adelaide of Austria, and of another in 1868 for the marriage of Umberto (I) and Princess Margaret of Savoy. During this exposition Princess Clotilde, wife of Napoleon's nephew (Napoleon, Count of Moncalieri), changed the Shroud's black cover of 1694 for a new one of crimson silk. As regards the exposition of 1842, our only in formation that this took place comes from a little article in a popular newspaper, according to which the intention had been to reproduce the Shroud in daguerreotype but the condition of the light and the dust – so it said! – kicked up by the crowd, prevented this from being done. We do not know what basis there was for this report even though contemporary, nor can we guess what results might have emerged. Given the process intended certainly not those revealed by the first photograph taken in 1898.

The great exposition of 1898

In this year an exposition was held for the marriage of Victor Emmanuel (III) and Helen of Montenegro. In point of fact, the marriage had taken place two years before but the exposition was postponed so as to coincide with celebrations for the religious centenaries being held in

Turin in 1898. Among the various anniversaries the most important were the four hundredth anniversary of the Cathedral, the 1500th anniversary of the Council of Turin, and the tercentenary of the founding of the Confraternities of the Most Holy Shroud and St Roch.

Turin Cathedral, rising on the area occupied in ancient times by three churches, was begun in 1491 and finally dedicated in honour of St John the Baptist in 1498. The architect was Meo da Caprina of Settignano, as is recorded on the stone set in the wall between the two windows of the facade.

The Council of Turin, in contrast, marks an important date in the history of the Diocese of Turin. Since it is not known when precisely the episcopal see of Turin was founded, the Council represents the earliest proof of its existence.

The Confraternity of the Most Holy Shroud, still in being and active today, was set up on May 25, 1598, and at that time cared for the mentally sick, for whose recovery it built the city's first psychiatric hospital. The Confraternity of St Roch, also still going strong, its original purpose being to bury the dead who had no one to bury them, was founded on September 7, that same year.

The centenaries were celebrated with a great Exhibition of Sacred Art forming part of the other event scheduled for that year in Turin: the General Italian Exhibition to mark the 50th anniversary of the granting of the Albertine Statute. The Exhibition of Sacred Art was a sort of victory for Piedmontese Catholicism, which intended by this to affirm its own presence and liveliness in a political context of uneasy coexistence.

The Exposition of the Shroud opened on the morning of May 25 and closed in the late afternoon of June 2. The total number of visitors was estimated at 800,000, half of whom came from outside Turin, in the course of nine part-days and 199 hours of exposition, with an average therefore of more than 95,000 persons per day.

The photograph that revealed the image on the Shroud

Meanwhile, in April 1898, a subcommittee of the Exhibition had been set up to deal with photography, whence to begin preparations for reproducing the Shroud while awaiting the Sovereign's permission – which however was not to be taken for granted, given the Royal House's mistrust and fear that there might be financial exploitation of it. Opposition was overcome once the necessary assurances had been guaranteed by the fact that Secondo Pia would be taking the photographs. Pia, a lawyer, described himself as an 'amateur photographer', not in the derogatory sense of the term but in the sense that to him photography was a passion, an amusement, not a profession. His fame as a very skilled photographer of the day was already widespread, particularly because of his many campaigns to document Piedmont's artistic and archaeological heritage.

Secondo Pia had very little time at his disposal for making his preparations and even less for taking his pictures. A first session took place on May 25 at 2 pm, a little before the cathedral doors were to open to inaugurate the pilgrimages, and a second on the evening of May 28. Pio had never seen the Shroud, nor could he know the exact conditions that he would be finding to work in. Counting on his vast experience in photographing pictures inside churches in very various but always inconvenient conditions, he decided to take a series of plates of different shapes and different timings, in the hope of obtaining at least one correct exposure. During the first session he took two test photographs (21 x 27 format) which in his own words were no good. From examination of the material in the Pia Archive however, we find that not only did these photographs come out but that in them the negative character of the Shroud imprint can be clearly seen. On the 28th he took a further two test pictures and afterwards the four definitive plates (format 50 x 60). In this second session Pia had to move his wooden scaffolding back from the Shroud on account of the reflections caused by the plate-glass temporarily installed in front of it. He had to hoist his bulky camera on to this scaffolding to get it to the same height as the altar. These plates have now been discovered and are now in the Museum of the Shroud in Turin.

Pia always regretted not having had the chance to take detailed pictures of the Shroud. The pictures of the face which were put into circulation are thus the enlargements of a detail from the complete plate. Their definition however is proof of Pia's great skill as a photographer.

Reactions in scientific circles

The discovery of the extraordinary face which appeared on the photographic negative caused some people to proclaim it a miracle, while contrariwise among others it aroused sceptical reactions, which soon turned to suspicions, polemics and finally open denigration in many sectors of the contemporary world. Doubts having been dispelled over procedural correctness, thanks to the undisputed serious-mindedness and ability of Secondo Pia, the event triggered off scientific study of the Shroud. For the discovery that there was a negative imprint on the Shroud, a concept born of the nineteenth century with the invention of photography, dealt a serious blow to the hypotheses of forgery based on the statements of Pierre d'Arcis. At last scholars were able to get their hands on an accurate reproduction of the Shroud, on which to carry out, in part at least, the much-needed direct studies to supplement historical research on which hitherto the question of authenticity had been based. One of the first people to be interested in the results of Pia's photography was the agnostic scientist Yves Delage, who became convinced of the Shroud's authenticity. This was not of religious consequence as far as he was concerned but led him to present a scientific report on the subject to the Paris Academy of Sciences of which he was a member: a report of the highest seriousness and clarity which still deserves great respect today for its honesty and rigour. His action instantly gave rise to a series of drawn-out polemics as the secular, rationalist, scientific world refused to accept not only his conclusions but the very possibility that anyone should stoop to reflect on and investigate an object so closely connected with religion. Delage's lecture bore very important fruit however, not least because his work was continued by a young assistant, Dr Paul Vignon, who for the next thirty years went on studying the Shroud under its various aspects, thus becoming the forefather of all modern sindonologists.

Giuseppe Enrie's photographs

In 1931 an exposition was held for the marriage of the Hereditary Prince Umberto of Savoy and Marid José of Belgium, and this provided another opportunity for having the Shroud photographed. The job was entrusted to a professional,

Giuseppe Enrie, who with more up-to-date apparatus and techniques obtained the fine photographs which are still in use today, and which, what is more, confirmed the accuracy of the results obtained by Pia. Two years later another exposition took place to mark the 1900th anniversary of the Redemption.

In 1939 the Shroud left Turin the second time. Transferred in great secrecy to the Sanctuary of Montevergine, there it stayed throughout the World War, hidden inside an altar.

Scientific research went on meanwhile, encouraged by the International Centre of Sindonology, founded in 1959 by archiepiscopal decree within the Confraternity of the Most Holy Shroud to continue the work of the *Cultores Sanctae Sindonis*.

The first official scientific Commission for studying and for carrying out direct examinations on the Shroud was summoned by Cardinal Michele Pellegrino in 1969, thence to proceed to a 'recognition' of the Shroud.

This was when the most recent official photographs were taken, including the first colour photographs by the photographer Giovanni Battista Judica Cordiglia.

The Shroud on TV in 1973 and the exposition of 1978

A televised exposition took place four years later, all the more memorable for a fine meditation by His Holiness Paul VI. It also gave the Swiss criminologist Max Frei an opportunity, using adhesive strips, to remove particles from the Shroud material, on which he was to complete his research leading to the identification of various kinds of pollen on the Shroud. At the same time, under the Commission's supervision, some threads were removed for haematological and microscopic tests and two scraps for research into the nature of the material itself.

The last public showing took place in 1978 to celebrate the 400th anniversary of the Shroud's translation to Turin. This was the longest exposition in memory, lasting from August 27 to October 8. On the two last days of the exposition, the Turin International Centre of Sindonolgy held an International Study Congress, the results of which form the basis of contemporary research on the Shroud.

When the exposition was over, the Shroud was made available to the scholars for a good 120 hours on end, so that it could be subjected to every non-destructive form of examination that might seem appropriate.

On April 13, 1980, during a visit to Turin, the present Pope John Paul II enjoyed a private exposition, and was thus the second pope in history to venerate the Shroud in person.

Radiocarbon dating in 1988

On April 21, 1988, samples were taken from the Shroud fabric for radiocarbon dating, the results of which, as is well-known, were to attribute the Shroud to the Middle Ages, and were announced on October 13, 1988.

In 1992 the Shroud was opened up again for a group of experts chosen by Cardinal Saldarini to check its condition and suggest appropriate action to guarantee its better conservation in time to come. Results of this inspection showed that the Shroud could no longer be kept rolled up as at present; a new method will have to be found for the Shroud to remain stretched out at full length. Since this does not seem possible in its historic Chapel without wrecking Guarini's peerless architecture, the Shroud will in all likelihood not go back to Bertola's altar, where in any case it has not been kept since 1993 when it was moved into the choir of Turin Cathedral to allow Guarini's Chapel to be restored.

The fire of April 11, 1997

The work restoring the Chapel to its original splendour was scarcely finished when it was, alas, brought to nothing by a very serious fire breaking out on the night of April 11-12, 1997. This badly damaged one wing of the Royal Palace, affecting the Chapel to the point perhaps of making it unstable and causing damage very hard to make good.

Luckily however the Shroud, not directly affected by the fire on account of its position, could be brought to safety without being damaged, though not without difficulty and danger.

Kept today in a place which for security reasons has not been revealed, the Shroud will next be displayed to the faithful at the 1998 exposition, celebrating the centenary of Pia's photograph and also commemorating the other events of 1898 mentioned above. A further exposition will be held in the year 2000 for the solemn Jubilee to close the millennium.

From the fourteenth century backwards: on the way to Europe

From Lirey, a journey in reverse

In the foregoing brief survey, we have traced the known history and chronicle of the Shroud to the present day.

Although we do not have such certain information in the period before the fourteenth century as we have in the centuries afterwards, this doesn't mean research has been given up. On the contrary, we should be aware that protracted investigations of all sorts suggest the possibility, we may say the very high probability, that the Shroud of Turin has an origin much more ancient than the Middle Ages.

At this point, historical disciplines have to plumb the period before the fourteenth century by light of what has already been ascertained by various types of scientific research: to make a critical evaluation of the information available, to clear the ground of irrelevant texts and references, to demonstrate inconsistencies and to explore any promising hypotheses that may emerge. These nuggets of information, in their turn, can become reference points for other people engaged in direct research, by directing them towards experimental testing of historical hypotheses about the Shroud's whereabouts.

In tackling the possible history of this period, we must not therefore expect any certainties: many people have hazarded all sorts of conclusions. Indeed, rather than a reconstruction of historical facts, the history of the 'dark' period might be better laid bare by means of a 'history of historiography', a history, that is to say, of the hypotheses advanced from the sixteenth century onwards to throw light on the Shroud's past. Here however we shall confine our attention to those hypotheses seemingly most widely held today and offering prospects for future research.

So back we go to Lirey, with our plan to make a journey in reverse.

The 'silence' of Geoffroy de Charny

Scholars have often emphasised that in the documents we possess, the de Charny family never give a clear explanation of how the Shroud came into their possession. This is certainly a point which might encourage one to think of a hoax on their part, forcing them to keep an embarrassed silence.

From our historical sources however we do know sufficiently well the kind of man Geoffroy de Charny was for us to be able to state with absolute certainty that he is above suspicion over any such sacrilegious forgery. He is of course placed in a bad light in Pierre d'Arcis's memorial – a pretty poisonous production although it does not accuse him directly – nor can we doubt from the tenor of the said documents that Geoffroy himself it was and not his relatives or descendants who endowed the Lirey church with the relic.

It is more acceptable to think the de Charnys had what they considered good reasons for not publicising the Shroud's provenance, and perhaps these reasons were connected with the Church's somewhat severe rules about recently rediscovered relics, governing their authenticity and trafficking in them. This vagueness – not to say secretiveness – over the Shroud's provenance has been the basis for several hypotheses about the route it took to reach Europe.

A Shroud in Constantinople in 1204

The starting point is 1204. For during the Fourth Crusade there is evidence of a Shroud's being located in Constantinople, the description of which could identify it with the one in Turin. We shall return to this subject in a minute. That Shroud was to disappear in the sack of the city by the Crusaders.

This could be an important *terminus* since records of the Shroud's later stay in Constantinople do not seem to be much in agreement. For instance, the transfer of a portion of Shroud by Baldwin II to Louis IX of France in 1247 does not presuppose the presence of the whole Shroud in Constantinople, but only a fragment of it, no description being given of what it was like. If however the Shroud actually was in Constantinople in 1204, we may very reasonably attribute its disappearance to the Crusaders.

Turning hence to the theories of how it found its way to Europe, today's historians for the most part favour one of two possibilities. One links the Shroud to the vicissitudes of the knights of the Temple of Solomon, better known as the Templars. The other envisages a stop in Greece.

Hypothesis of the Templars

To the historian Ian Wilson we owe the reconstruction according to which the Shroud came into the Templars' hands after the sack of Constantinople and they then guarded it in their fortresses.

The powerful Order was founded to defend the passage of pilgrims from Jaffa to Jerusalem and began its work there in 1118-1119. Its rule – a very strict one – was drawn up a few years later by St Bernard. The knights fought boldly during their stay in the East, too boldly for some historians, who see in their intemperate actions one of the causes contributing to the fall of the Latin Kingdom of Jerusalem.

Driven out of the East, they settled in the West where, having given up their warrior commitment, they engaged in intense economic activity, which had already made them a power with considerable wealth. This wealth was probably the spring releasing the mechanism for the Order's destruction.

On October 13, 1307, by order of the King of France, Philip the Fair, all the knights then on the soil of the Kingdom of France were arrested and charged with having committed shameful crimes and even of having abandoned the faith for idolatry. More probably it was their economic power that excited the king's greed.

Under threat of execution but also owing to merciless torture, many confessed their alleged guilt, even though no material proof was forthcoming. At the end of the ecclesiastical investigation into the Order, Pope Clement V pronounced its suppression on April 3, 1312, as an interim measure, without however uttering sentence of condemnation. Verdict of guilt as regards individuals was by no means unanimous, and while in the countries subject to French influence it was accepted, in England and other countries the Templars were acquitted.

On March 18, 1314, in Paris, the last act: despite the perplexity of the ecclesiastical representatives and before they could give their judgement, by order of Philip the Fair, the Grand Master Jacques de Molay was burnt at the stake.

In these happenings, Wilson finds certain elements which he thinks may concern the history of the Shroud. With Jacques de Molay was burnt the Master of Normandy, a certain Geoffroy de Charnay. Furthermore, at Templecombe in southwest England, where there used to be a Templar centre, an oak panel-painting has been found, seemingly at one time the lid of a chest, decorated with the picture of a bearded head reminiscent of the one on the Shroud.

Difficulties and weak points in the Templar theory

Wilson concludes that the famous idol the Templars were supposed to have worshipped was none other than the Shroud, and that it passed to the de Charny family, after the Order was suppressed, by means of the Geoffroy whose surname is virtually identical and who was burnt at the stake. The theory is very attractive but caution is needed, for at present it has not been conclusively proved that there is any relationship between the two Geoffroys. The similarity of the name, always admitting the uncertainty of medieval spelling, does not give us the right to tamper with known pedigrees. We should also bear in mind that in time past other French families are on record as having borne the place-name Charny as their surname.

Then, the presence of the Templecombe panel and other cross-references to the face on the Shroud, though very intriguing , can however be accounted for by awareness of the *Mandylion* of Edessa, renowned for its unrivalled miraculous power of protecting in battle. We may even think that in all likelihood the accusation of idolatry was only a device of the King's to justify his issuing the order for the Templars' arrest.

This said, we do not mean to rule out a possible role for the Templars in the Shroud's progress to Europe. Other historians have also advanced theories in connection with the Order though on different lines, and I myself have found in a late manuscript a hint about Templar activity in the matter. Even so the theory thus formulated, all the serious research notwithstanding, leaves much in doubt.

A letter to the Pope

The second theory, which was already being aired at the beginning of our century on the basis of somewhat fragile evidence, has today acquired new elements to interest us.

At the National Congress of Sindonology held in Bologna in 1981 a document was presented containing the transcript of a letter from Theodore Angelus Comnenus (brother of Michael Angelus, of the family of the deposed Emperor of Constantinople) to Pope Innocent III. Immediately after the fall of Constantinople, the Despotate of Epirus was set up, under the rule of Michael Angelus. It consisted of the territories on the northwest coast of Greece, its capital was Arta; this became the rallying point for all who refused to submit to the Latins.

In the letter dated August 1, 1205, Theodore, writing in his brother's name and in his own, denounces the Crusaders' pillaging of Constantinople and in particular laments the loss of the 'most sacred' of the relics: 'the sheet in which our Lord Jesus Christ was wrapped after his death and before his resurrection', which was then being kept in Athens.

The document is extremely interesting, even though of course we cannot be absolutely sure that the Shroud named in it was the same as the one in Turin. Furthermore this letter formed part of a 'cartulary', that is to say a collection of copies of documents, and this unfortunately got destroyed in Naples during the Second World War. So today we only possess a nineteenth century transcript of certain passages, among which is the one of interest to us. Hence therefore it is impossible for us to conduct a direct examina-

tion of the document itself and we have only its
claimed provenance and content to rely on.

As to its substance, the letter is plausible, since
it fits well into the context of reaction to the
abuses committed by the Crusaders, which were
recognised and censured by Pope Innocent.

A series of signposts for drawing a panorama

From the point of view of research on the Shroud
itself, the letter also fits well into a series of clues
and references which, taken as individual items,
do not make much sense but, when put together,
offer a complex and rather suggestive panorama.

For it is possible, having been carried off from
Constantinople, that the Shroud passed through
Greece and thence reached Europe through chan-
nels not yet clear. Papal sanctions on the trafficking in Constantinopolitan relics could account
for documentary reticence about this, but the
whole topic needs to be gone into in greater
depth.

We must not forget that ancient traditions
speak of a Shroud's having been brought to
Europe – the one preserved at Besançon and later
destroyed in the French Revolution, certainly a
copy of the one in Turin – by a crusader with a
name familiar to us, Otto La Roche, who held
the lordship of Athens after the fall of Constantinople. But in the de Charny pedigree too there

are connections with families who had a role in Greece. What is more, some of the more fanciful theories constructed over the centuries to account for the Shroud's arrival in Europe can be shown to contain basic elements explicable on the hypothesis that the Shroud had journeyed through Greece.

Fragment of Robert de Clary's text in which he attests the presence of a Shroud in Constantinople in 1204.

Constantinople

Testimony of a crusader

I mentioned the existence a little earlier of testimony witnessing to the presence of the Shroud in Constantinople in 1203-04. This is found in the writings of a crusader, certainly a minor figure who would have been forgotten long ago were it not for the description he has left us of his stay in Constantinople during the Fourth Crusade.

An anomalous crusade which, aiming to fight in Egypt, the nerve-centre of Moslem power, was launched by the Venetians initially to restore the Republic's authority at Zara – which was taken and sacked in 1202 – and then at Constantinople, the Pope's irresolution notwithstanding, to restore Isaac II to the throne, he having been ousted by his brother Alexius III.

The crusaders entered Constantinople peacefully the first time after a short siege, once a popular rising had put Isaac back on the throne. This was in July 1203. For a few months the crusaders lived encamped out side the city gates, maintaining rather strained relations with the Emperor and the Greek inhabitants. It was however during this period that they were able to visit the city which they could see was rich and luxurious. But now a new popular disturbance deposed the Emperor, replacing him with the leader of the nationalist movement Alexius V Ducas. The crusaders then attacked the city and took it on April 12, 1204. The capital of the empire was engulfed in flames and subjected to a comprehensive sacking.

Then it was, according to Robert de Clary, that the Shroud disappeared 'in which our Lord was wrapped, which stood upright every Friday so that the figure of our Lord could be plainly seen there. No one, either Greek or French, ever knew what became of their *sydoine* (i.e. Shroud) after the city was taken'.

This is an intriguing reference in that it gives us a fairly precise account of a wide piece of cloth containing the complete image of Christ and mentioning the wrapping of the corpse in words very similar to those in the description Theodore Angelus was later to give of it.

Nicholas Mesarites, keeper of the relics

But this is not the only, though the clearest, evidence of the presence of a Shroud in Constantinople. Earlier, in 1201, Nicholas Mesarites, keeper of the relics at the Chapel of St Mary of the Pharos, while defending the church from a group of rioters, admonished them, reminding them of the sacredness of the place and what it contained. Among the relics of the passion there preserved, he cited the burial cloths of Christ 'which wrapped the Ineffable One, dead, naked and perfumed after his passion', which made the place peculiarly sacred since 'here (in this chapel) Christ rises again and the *sindon* and burial linens are the proof of it'. This is another piece of evidence which does not have as much relevance when taken by itself as when in conjunction with Robert de Clary's text and Theodore's letter.

A turning point in the iconography of Christ's burial

There is more however. Père Dubarle, the author of an indispensable critical text on the history of the Shroud until the Constantinople period, points out the importance of iconography in integrating tradition with the written word. He emphasises that contemporaneously with the evidence for the presence of the Shroud in Constantinople with the complete image of Christ's body, a new iconographical departure occurs in representations of Christ's burial, into which the use of a large burial sheet is now introduced.

A very interesting example of this type of innovation, with features suggesting there may have been knowledge of the Shroud, is to be found in a miniature in the Pray Codex in Budapest, especially with reference to the positioning of Christ's body, certain anatomical features and the presence of a very long winding-sheet. In the picture of the meeting of the Holy Women with the Angel at the tomb, it would indeed seem the artist meant to reproduce the herringbone weave of the Shroud, and some people have also claimed to see the signs characteristic of an earlier fire than that of Chambéry on the Pray shroud. To explain the strange place for the manuscript to be, which dates back to the end of the twelfth century, we recall that King Bela III of Hungary had been educated at the court of Byzantium so that he could become emperor. Owing to the birth of a legitimate heir however, this was not to be.

Without wanting to force the interpretation, it seems impossible to deny there had been some object influencing the depiction of Christ's burial in a particular way and coinciding with the supposed presence of the Shroud in Constantinople.

Then there are also many minor sources bearing witness to the presence of Christ's burial effects in Constantinople towards the end of the eleventh century. Historians have tried to

Pray mss Fol.27v preserved in the National Library, Budapest. The picture is divided into two parts. Above, the anointing; below, the visit of the Holy Women to the sepulchre (end of twelfth century). Source: Ian Wilson, The Turin Shroud. London 1978.

pinpoint the time when this tradition began. In many ways this has involved a one-item agenda, an attempt, that is to say, to find confirmation for a theory developed by Ian Wilson, linking the Shroud to the venerable image of Edessa, the *Holy Mandylion*, to which we have already referred several times.

The Holy Mandylion, twelfth century fresco (Spas Nereditsa, near Novgorod).

The Mandylion of Odessa

A revolution in studies on the Shroud

At this point we need to pause briefly over the Image of Edessa, if we are to grasp this hypothesis revolutionising studies in Shroud history. This may be done directly by offering a possible solution to the historical problem of where the Shroud was for the first one thousand years, or, above all, indirectly by stimulating scholarly efforts to assess its reliability. Thus two new lines of research have opened up which, due mainly to the work of the aforementioned Wilson and Dubarle, to whom we should now add Gino Zaninotto, have yielded a magnificent harvest of references and texts which are striking to say the least.

It is not easy to trace the career of this picture of Christ's face. Its origin, its reputation and its very existence are shrouded in legend and entwined with the stories of other pictures of Christ's face that have appeared in the course of Christian history. Behind the hypotheses however there may well be a truth to be uncovered.

The legend of an exchange of letters between Jesus and the King of Edessa

At the origin of the *Mandylion* is the legend of an exchange of letters between Jesus and Abgar V, King of Edessa, who being sick asked Jesus to come and cure him. In other sources the legend is expanded where, for Jesus's letter, an oral response is substituted, containing a promise of impregnability too for the city of Edessa and accompanied by a tablet on which Hannan, the King's archivist and painter, sent by Abgar to Jesus, had painted Jesus's portrait (*Doctrine of Addai*, fourth or sixth century).

A reworking of this text makes further changes to the story. Besides carrying the letter, Abgar's envoy had the specific task of observing what Jesus looked like, obviously with a view to describing him and making a picture. But because he did not succeed in getting the basic features right, Jesus himself asked for a towel. He was given a piece of cloth *folded four times* (*tetradiplon*). Having washed, he wiped his face and on the cloth remained the imprint of his face (*Acts of Thaddaeus*, second half of sixth or early seventh century). I have italicised the curious expression *tetradiplon* since it is in great part responsible for the birth of the theory about the Shroud which we are now going to examine. For Wilson pointed out that the Shroud, when folded four times, becomes a rectangle in the centre of which the face alone appears. Some ancient reproductions of the *Mandylion* do indeed show us a rectangle with the longer side as base, covered with diamond shaped trelliswork, with a central medallion from which the face emerges. On photographs of the Shroud, traces have been observed, perhaps attributable to this ancient folding into four that we have just mentioned.

A tradition older than the fourth century

The tradition of the existence of a portrait of Christ is hence very ancient – earlier than the fourth century – even though very nebulous in form, and the period and circumstances of its arrival in Edessa far from clear. Also, there is a reciprocal borrowing of elements and references from other pictures of Christ's face. The tradition of the Veronica immediately springs to mind.

Equally it is hard to follow development of the history of the image of Edessa which, for a period, disappears completely from descriptions of the city. It reappears in a chronicle of the

Persian siege in AD 544, written by Evagrius Scholasticus some fifty years after the event. In this the image of the Face is mentioned again, this time described as 'not made by human hand' – the term that had come into use for images miraculously imprinted without human agency – which when carried on the battlefield routed the enemy troops with unquenchable fire. Not by chance is this the period when, as we have seen, the *Acts of Thaddaeus* re-work the earlier version of the *Doctrine of Addai* in miraculistic form.

Later, yet another tradition was to be added: that the image had been miraculously rediscovered in a niche in the city wall where it had been hidden centuries before, which would explain the silence of the earlier sources.

Legendary matter aside, certain it is that specifically during the sixth century a remarkable typology of Christ's face became established. Thenceforth the *Mandylion* was destined to proceed in triumph towards universal fame. Evidence of this are the many texts that mention it. For one particular reason too: the iconoclastic crisis broke out, condemning the cult of images as a pagan habit. Among those defenders of its legitimacy as an ancient Christian tradition, many were to recall as one of the major examples – if not the greatest of all – the valour and uninterrupted devotion aroused by the Image of Edessa, and in this sense it was also to be cited at the Second Council of Nicaea (AD 787). A sufficiently clear sign that this image presented characteristics superior to all other supposed portraits of Christ then venerated in the East.

The Mandylion reaches Constantinople

This reputation, respected even by the Arabs who occupied the city in AD 639, was evidently the goad prompting the Emperor of Byzantium to desire the so-greatly venerated image for his own, in the city that had become the greatest reliquary in the world. In AD 944, after a siege, the *Mandylion* was handed over by the Arab Emir to the Byzantine General John Curcuas, despite insurrection on the part of the Christians of Edessa, who not only stopped fighting but actually granted notable favours to the besieged Arabs.

Taken on board ship, the *Mandylion* reached Constantinople on August 15, to be welcomed with great pomp by the imperial court.

The *Mandylion* has now completed its journey to Constantinople, bringing us back to the moment when we had left the Byzantine capital. It is from this very date that the first references to the presence of the Lord's Shroud in Constantinople begin. But the strange thing is that some texts of this epoch refer to the fact that the *Mandylion* is not a picture of Christ at any moment of his earthly life but one directly linked to his Passion. A homily ordered by Constantine VII Porphyrogenitus – co-emperor in AD 944 – or possibly even composed by him, describes the face as due to 'a liquid secretion without colouring matter or painter's art', and points to a tradition (already gathered by Gregory the Referendary) holding that the image had been formed by the bloody sweat of Gethsemane.

Not the image of a face only, but of the whole body

The image is described as evanescent, hard to read. But other texts give us to think (and some are absolutely explicit) that in that cloth there is not only a face, but the wound in the side can be seen, and that it bears the imprint of the whole body. Let one sermon stand for all: I quote from one preserved in a tenth century codex, in which Jesus's letter to Abgar is significantly modified. The Lord writes that he had sent a cloth on which could be seen 'the image not only of my face but the length of my whole body divinely transformed'. The sermon goes on to explain how this impression has come about: Jesus 'prostrated himself full length on very white linen, and so by divine power the most beautiful likeness not only of the face, but also of the whole body of the Lord was impressed upon the cloth'. But other testimony may lead us to think that, even in the Edessan period, some people already knew the 'secret' of the *Mandylion*.

Hence we find ourselves facing a hypothesis

which, while not containing anything definite, is certainly suggestive. A face of Jesus, known from a period quite close to that of the Gospels, which from being a painting comes to be described as not made by human hand. Naturally theological controversies may have influenced this development, but it cannot be ruled out that a more careful examination of the image has taken place and changed the way it is to be interpreted. Examination which must have revealed that besides the representation of a face there was that of a body too. An image theoretically formed during the passion and caused by the Lord's sweat and blood. All these elements certainly cannot be used as proof positive that the Shroud of Turin existed before the year AD 1000. They should not however be dismissed with contempt or indifference. As always, research requires balance, and extreme positions do not favour the requisite judgmental calm.

An image as the basis of icongraphy of Christ

This theory is linked to a fact which Paul Vignon was already emphasising in his day and which other scholars have gone into more deeply since. If we look carefully into the development of the iconography of Christ, we observe that at a certain point, after some fluctuations partly due to the influence of pagan representations of the deity, it assumes a characteristic type which then runs right through Christian history up to our own day: a Christ, bearded, oval faced, with long hair hanging down to his shoulders. But in ancient representations and in the traditional image of the icons, there are other recurrent motifs too, somewhat anomalous ones indeed, which have now been painstakingly catalogued: the large eyes, the prominent cheekbones, the triangle between the eyebrows, the characteristic lock of hair in the middle of the forehead – these are some of them.

Vignon thought (and what he thought now many an art historian thinks too) that this model goes back to an archetype displacing all others by virtue of its credibility and fame. Certainly the Face of Edessa – at least as we know it from ancient representations since the real thing vanished in Constantinople – is well qualified to be one of the most ancient representations to display these characteristics, and its appearance coincides exactly with the general adoption of this model in Christian iconography as mentioned above. All these characteristics can however be checked off on the image of the Shroud face, where some details on the tortured face of the corpse would certainly have been modified by an artist, especially when we consider that Holy Faces were meant to depict a living man. Thus, the swollen cheekbones could have been interpreted as prominent ones, the trickle of blood on the forehead as a lock of hair, and so forth.

Abgar of Edessa receives the Mandylion (Source: K. Weitzmann, The Monastery of St Catherine at Mount Sinai, *Princetown 1976).*

Objections to the Edessa theory

Of course the Edessa theory has its weak points too and objections have been advanced that need considering. We wonder for instance what the reason could have been for only wanting to display the face, when the whole body could be seen. It is not out of place to consider perhaps that this might have led to misunderstandings, at the same time arousing polemics between the various doctrinal schools agitating the Church.

Be that as it may, the representations of the *Mandylion* known to us – and it could not be otherwise – only show the face.

We must then consider that, even accepting that Shroud and *Mandylion* are one and the same, the period before any evidence of its presence in Edessa still remains obscure. The argument from silence however does not necessarily lead to negative conclusions about its prior existence. We shall have to be content however with the tradition, going back to the early centuries, according to which Christ's funerary linens were not lost. A very ancient witness to this may be a passage, often recurring in Shroud literature, in the apocryphal gospel *according to the Hebrews*.

The Edessa theory has a wide following among writers favourable to the Shroud and, since its journey through Turkey can be objectively checked by identifying the various pollen grains present on the sheet, that would vouch for a stay in the geographical area of Edessa (modern Urfa or Sanliurfa). On the significance of the pollen grains however I refer the reader to the relevant booklet in this series dealing with botanical research on the Shroud.

In sindonological circles, the Edessa theory has completely supplanted earlier, very transient ones which held that the Shroud had been preserved in Jerusalem, then transferred to Constantinople, and next even moved to Rome. Such theories were based essentially on an interpretation of those various sources we have already mentioned. But these, at most, allow us to state that in the early centuries of Christianity it was generally known that Christ's burial linens had been preserved.

Conclusions

The distance covered

Together in these pages we have made a journey through history, possibly leading us from the tomb of Jesus to Turin. In so doing, our aim has been to make our contribution to the vexed question of the Shroud's origin. In tackling the problem of its authenticity – in the sense of making sure that it agrees with the tradition that maintains it to be the winding-sheet used for Jesus' burial – we realise that the Shroud's presence and availability favour results of tests directly carried out on it.

In support there is research into and critical examination of all those sources which may serve to increase our indirect knowledge about the

Shroud, such as exegesis of the gospel texts, history, iconography and so forth. If then from a strictly historical point of view we are not in a position to formulate such precise reconstructions as would lead us back from Turin to the time of Jesus, there is no need for us to think research on the Shroud has reached a dead-end, especially when we consider the notable acquisitions accumulated by direct examination in recent years.

We have seen it is easy to trace its history back to the fourteenth century. For there are no appreciable gaps or such as would admit a doubt that some sort of manipulation could have taken place during the period. The greatest precautions have always surrounded the Shroud, and no one doubts that the Shroud of Turin is the same one as was argued over at Lirey in the second half of the fourteenth century. In any case, a pilgrim badge found in the Seine in Paris displaying the coats-of-arms of de Charny and de Vergy (the latter being the family of Geoffroy I's second wife) and hence undoubtedly going back to that period, bears the image of the unfolded Shroud – the earliest actually known to us – which is certainly the Shroud of Turin, with remarkable definition of the image and of the herringbone weave of the cloth.

The focus moves from the historical to the scientific plane

The Lirey period is documented as a certainly critical moment in the Shroud's history, but the documents we actually have are not in themselves enough to prove that the Shroud is not authentic. Indeed the results of about a hundred years of direct research do not seem compatible with Pierre d'Arcis's assertions, whereas the results of carbon-14 dating would contrariwise seem to strengthen their value. Hence argument is shifting into the scientific field and not the other way round, and the experts in carbon-dating, the chemists and the physicists will now have to make the evaluations that we need.

The real historical problems in the objective sense of the word, lie in reconstructing the earlier period. It is clear, this research into a history predating the Middle Ages is a one-item agenda, and this can easily attract the accusation of being undertaken solely to justify veneration of a supposed relic. It is nonetheless legitimate for all that, and I think it not only necessary but actually a duty to make the effort. The real historical error lies in thinking the matter was closed with the legal proceedings at Lirey. On the contary one may get bogged down by over-valuing what are only working hypotheses. To sum up, the objective (at least for this writer) is to weigh up whether there is in fact total darkness before the medieval period as regards preservation and veneration of the Lord's Shroud, or whether there are elements allowing and encouraging us to continue our researches, knowing it will not be history alone that gives us all the answers we await from the Shroud.

The value of a long tradition

I think we may grant that a tradition exists that relics of Jesus were preserved, among which were his burial linens. There is also a constant iconographical tradition which could be plausibly accounted for by knowledge of the Shroud image. We recall that documents – in the technical sense – are not only those written down but everything that can provide us with information about a fact. On the basis then of a substantial body of references and evidence, painstakingly extracted from the most ancient sources – but which while extremely suggestive cannot be regarded as conclusive – hypotheses have been drawn up indicating the lines of investigation to be pursued and, perhaps more important still, how the past of the Shroud of Turin may be reconstructed.

For, since it is not a total 'silence', we cannot yield to the temptation of setting historical research aside, in the broadest sense of the term, that is to say. It is essential, and its conclusions and even its doubts are a valuable contribution to other disciplines studying the Shroud, and vice-versa. We only need to think about the importance a reconstruction of the exact events of the fire of 1532 may have for evaluating the potential errors over carbon-dating, or on the historical contribution derived from research into micro-traces on the Shroud.

An object with no history whatever could hardly

hold one's interest for long. An object with a disputed but possible history is a fascinating challenge for the historian, but for the scientist too. And it is a challenge, together with all those others the Shroud throws down, that we must face.

Hence we can only say that at present, from a strictly historical point of view, there are no conclusive elements for confirming the tradition of its authenticity or for denying it.

This, it seems to me, is the conclusion to be drawn from these few pages. Pages which I naturally do not claim to be exhaustive but in which I have tried my best to summarise the elements of an investigation costing incredible effort but even so only just beginning. Alas, I have had to skip over many facts and events that, with more space, could have furnished a more complete picture.

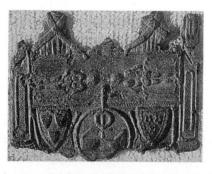

Pilgrim badge recovered from the Seine and bearing the first image of the Shroud of Lirey – Turin; today in the Musée de Cluny, Paris. (Source: I. Wilson, The Turin Shroud, *London 1978).*